Adorned with True Beauty

A Study of 1 Peter
for Wise Women

Kay Daigle

Adorned with True Beauty

ISBN: 0-7375-0124-3
ISBN13: 978-0-7375-0124-7
Biblical Studies Press
Richardson, Texas

Adorned with True Beauty

Introduction

We women are so busy these days! If your life is anything like mine, you have more commitments than you know how to handle. There are family, church, and community responsibilities that you must juggle. As you open this Bible study, you may be thinking, "How will I ever have time to make it through these lessons?" And yet you know that God promises to bless the study of His Word. You know that your relationship with Him should be a priority in your life. My prayer for you and for me is that God will so draw us to Himself that we will not miss a day of time with Him in His Word. I pray that He will do a mighty work in all of our lives as we spend the next few weeks together.

As I write this study, I can see in my mind's eye a variety of women who need to know that they are precious to God; I can imagine women of all stages of life desiring to adorn themselves with the inner beauty that God desires for them. I see singles, young married women, mothers, grandmothers, and women at home and in the workplace wanting to share in the community of a small group of women who will accept them and love them. If you are ready to grow in the Scriptures and in relationships with others and with God, you are in the right place.

We are all on a journey with God through this life. Some of us are farther along than others. Yet, we join together each week throughout this study to become one community of women seeking to know their God. The exchange of thoughts in a small group of women of all ages has been one of the greatest blessings of my life. When I was young, I learned so much from the life stories of the women who had walked before me. Now I hope that the story of my journey will be encouraging to you. As you will notice, I share a lot of myself when I write a Bible study so that you will know that I am real.

May the Lord richly bless you as you commit to these nine weeks in fellowship with God and with other women, seeking to follow God and grow in our love for Him -

Kay Daigle

How to Use this Study Guide

This study is designed to help you consistently spend time in God's Word daily. Each week's lesson is divided into five days of homework so that you spend time with God listening to His voice each day. The Bible is God's message to you, and He wants to speak with you personally. You will gain the most from this study if you do it day by day, answering just that day's questions, rather than trying to stuff it all in at once. Working on it daily will also allow you to meditate upon what you have seen as you go about your other routines.

A Precious Word from God - Each week you will have a verse to memorize that brings out an essential lesson or thought from the week's study. Begin learning it the first day. You might copy it on an index card and carry it with you throughout the week, hiding God's Word in your heart.

Specific types of questions

Sharing questions - These questions are designed for you to write stories, insights, and applications from your own life. If we are to be in community with one another and support one another, we must truly know one another. Although you will never be forced to share one of these answers, be willing to be open and vulnerable with your small group by volunteering. Because we are all still growing and learning, we need each other's support.

Responding to God - On these questions, you are asked to write out a response to God after studying His Word to you. I have found that writing out my prayers helps me to focus better on what I need to say to God and gives me a way to review my prayers later. Be honest and open here as well. No one will call on you to read yours. You may desire to volunteer to share what you have written and should always feel free to do that.

- *Diamonds in the Word* - These questions are designed for those who want to dig deeper into God's Word. Some of these will be easy for even a beginning Bible student to answer, and some will require more experience in God's Word. As a group you will not discuss these, but the background that you gain from digging into God's Word in a deeper way will certainly enrich your own relationship with God if you apply what you study.

Personal Stories

Each lesson includes a true story that relates the truths of that week's lesson to a woman's real life experience. Some of the names have been changed to protect the guilty! Be sure and read these stories each week although your group may not have time to discuss them together. The stories themselves will be an encouragement to you in your walk with God and your growth in true beauty.

Adorned with True Beauty

Table of Contents

Week One ....*Adorned with the Beauty of Faith*.................... 9

Week Two ....*Adorned with Beauty through Trials* 19

Week Three ...*Adorned with Beauty through God's Word*.....31

Week Four ......*Adorned with the Beauty of Holiness*..............45

Week Five ....*Adorned with Beauty among Unbelievers*........61

Week Six ....*Adorned with the Beauty of a Gentle and Quiet Spirit*.................................. 73

Week Seven ...*Adorned with Beauty in Unjust Suffering* 87

Week Eight.....*Adorned with Beauty, Knowing the End Is Near* 99

Week Nine ......*Adorned with the Beauty of Humility* 111

Week One: Adorned with the Beauty of Faith

A Precious Word from God

"Charm is deceitful and beauty is fleeting,
but a woman who fears the Lord will be praised."
Proverbs 31:30 (NET)

Introduction

As you begin this first lesson, realize that you are precious to God, and as His daughter, He wants you to be adorned internally, not just externally, for true beauty resides in the heart. Each week we will focus on an aspect of true beauty from the book of 1 Peter. Do you have a desire to be so beautiful that everyone notices? More and more as the years pass, your character rather than your looks will attract others. As our memory verse this week explains, beauty is vain - meaning temporary like a vapor. I have found that to be all too true as I age. Without inward beauty, I have no beauty left!

Before you start the first day's lesson, take the time to ask God to bless your time with Him, to give you insight and understanding of His Word, and to help you walk with Him more intimately than ever before as a result of this study. Don't forget to memorize our verse!

Day One Study

If you can, **read through the entire book of 1 Peter** as if you had just received it in the mail. It is a letter from Peter to first-century believers. Have the following questions in mind as you read so that you can write today's answers as you go.

1. Note any initial thoughts that you have as you read. What is God saying that is meaningful to you where you are right now in your life?

2. Do you notice any repeated thoughts or ideas? If so, record them.

If you were not already familiar with this book, you may be surprised by the content. It is not a book about beauty, but in a sense you can see the whole book in that light. As we grow as believers, we should reflect more and more the beauty of Jesus, and this book helps us understand how to do that.

3. Responding to God: Write a prayer asking God to change you through this study into a truly beautiful woman in His eyes.

- *Diamonds in the Word* -For those of you who want to dig deeper into the diamonds of God's word, work on a book chart, if you know how to make one, or an outline of the flow of this book. Consider the repeated thoughts and ideas that you found, and use them to find the book theme. This is a whole week's assignment!

Day Two Study

The first and most important part of being truly beautiful is being adorned with faith. You may be just beginning to explore the meaning of faith, or you may have been on the journey of faith for many years. Wherever you are and whatever your background, this week's lesson will be helpful in seeing that to be truly beautiful, faith is essential.

Read 1 Peter 1:1-21. We are going to focus on only some of these verses this week and then dig into the others next week, but by reading them all, you will get them in context.

4. According to the first verse, Peter identifies the people to whom he sends this letter as strangers or aliens. How is a person of faith like an alien in a foreign land, or even a foreign world?

5. Read Phil. 3:20-21. What truths does Paul keep in mind that help him value heaven more than this world?

6. *Sharing question*: Consider your own life. Do you share Paul's hope? How does your life reflect the fact that your citizenship is not here? Name one specific way in which someone may see that in your life. (I know that this is your first lesson with your group and you do not know these other women well, but this is a safe place and we need to be open and honest with one another.) If you are more attached to this world than heaven, ask God for one practical way that you can grow in your love for Him and His kingdom, write it below, and be prepared to share it with your group.

You may have noticed that in 1 Peter 1:1-2 Peter describes those who receive this letter as not only strangers or aliens but also as chosen. There are entire books written about the truth that God has selected His children. God has decided not to reveal more than the fact that we are chosen. Instead of debating how this works, I would like you to think about how it feels to be chosen. Perhaps as a student you usually made the athletic teams. Maybe your job experience has been one of feeling chosen by a boss or company to tackle a specific task. We all have experienced times when we were picked and times when we weren't.

7. Read Romans 3:10-18. How are you described here? Be specific!

Clearly, we are not beautiful naturally. We are stained and ugly because of our sins; thus, by faith alone are we able to become beautiful in God's sight. Despite the ugliness of your sins, God has chosen you to be His daughter. His choice has nothing to do with your being better than anyone else, which this passage in Romans makes clear. He chose you in His mercy simply because He loves you and wants a relationship with you. I often hear people say that God loves you just the way you are, but that is not exactly correct. God loves you ***despite*** the way you are! If you truly believe that God selected you regardless of what He knew about you rather than because of it, you recognize how undeserving you are of God's mercy.

8. Responding to God: Write a prayer thanking God for His great love and mercy and for choosing you despite the fact that you did not deserve it.

I had a difficult time believing that God chose me - it didn't seem fair and I couldn't comprehend it. I was willing to accept only those things that I could wrap my mind around and embrace. Yet, the Bible clearly said that God chose His children. How could I believe that? But I went to God and asked Him to open my mind to the truth whether I understood it or not. Over time, I began to acknowledge this as true. I still cannot explain it and would never attempt to reconcile it with the truth that we are responsible to believe. To do so would be adding to God's word an explanation that He never gave. I have just accepted it by faith, and it has made me so much more aware of the mercies of

God in my life. I wasn't wise enough or smart enough to choose Him; He chose me despite me!

- *Diamonds in the Word* -Read Romans 9:6-18. What examples does Paul use here to explain the truth that God's choice is not because of our present or future actions? How can these verses help someone accept the truth that God selects His children?

Day Three Study

Who is Jesus? Becoming a Christian means that you become a follower of Jesus. He is *the* essential of our faith. If we are to adorn ourselves with faith, we must first know who Jesus is and what He has done for us. Many of you have already trusted in Him and if so, ask God to take your lesson today and help you fall more in love with Jesus than ever before as you are reminded of His great love for you.

Reread 1 Peter 1:1-21 to get back into the context of the verses.

9. What do you learn about Jesus from vv. 3, 18-21?

10. In order to recognize Jesus for who He really is, look up the following verses about Him. Note what you learn about Jesus' identity from the people who knew Him:

    a. Matt. 16:13-17

    b. John 1:1-3, 14

    c. John 1:29-30

d. John 4:42

11. Read 1 Corinthians 15:3-8. This is the good news, the gospel. What truths about Jesus does it involve?

Imagine how exciting it must have been to see Jesus alive again after His terrible death on a cross! His friends had lost all hope, forgetting what they had learned about His identity and not understanding the necessity for His death. Seeing Jesus alive totally changed their lives. When we believe, it should change us as well.

12. Read John 20:31. What are we to do with the truths about Jesus that we have seen in this lesson? What do we receive at that point?

13. Read John 14:6. Record Jesus' words below. What other options did Jesus give people for acquiring eternal life in heaven?

14. *Sharing question*: If you are a follower of Jesus Christ, summarize your story of how and when you came to believe in Him and trust Him as your personal Savior.

If you have never trusted Jesus to forgive you of your sins and to give you eternal life with Him, today is a wonderful time to do that. Call upon Him, believing that He is God's Son who died on your behalf to pay the penalty for your sins and rose again from the dead, and desiring a personal relationship with Him as God's daughter. Share your faith with your group or leader. Read His promise to you in Romans 10:13.

Day Four Study

Reread 1 Peter 1:3-5.

15. Once you are born again, what do you receive according to 1 Peter 1:4?

16. What guarantees that your entrance into heaven is absolutely secure (1 Peter 1:5)?

17. How does Romans 11:29 help you understand the security of your salvation?

18. Responding to God: Based on 1 Peter 1:3-5 and Day Four Lesson, write a prayer thanking Jesus for your salvation and the inheritance that you now have because of His death and resurrection. You might want to take some of the phrases from these verses and reword them into a prayer.

19. *Sharing question*: Do you have a friend who needs to know that Jesus died for her sins? Write down a specific way that you plan to show her the love of Christ and share with her the news that she can have the inheritance of heaven.

Day Five Study

20. Copy Proverbs 31:30 below, our "Precious Word from God" for this week, and memorize it.

Fearing the Lord means in a practical sense that you trust Him, knowing that you are accountable to Him, realizing that you must fall upon His mercy. We have seen in our study this week that we are all sinners before a holy God. Only by His forgiveness through Jesus' death for our sins are we able to enter into a family relationship with Him. As we trust Him, God begins to change us.

21. *Sharing question*: Does your life reflect the beauty of your faith? Write down one practical way in which your faith has changed you into a more beautiful woman.

Jerry's Story

At the age of probably six or seven I "walked the aisle" at the little country church that I grew up in. I followed in baptism. No one counseled with me about what it really meant and the steps one needed to take to give her life to Christ. I just remember thinking that it was neat that I was going to be baptized and that I would now be able to take the Lord's Supper whenever it was offered. I certainly didn't understand the meaning of that ordinance!

My husband was ordained as a deacon when I was in my mid twenties. The ordination committee came to our house to talk to us and asked me for my testimony. I realized then for the first time that I really didn't have a testimony, but I was too proud to admit it and made up a pretty convincing one. The Lord didn't let go of me. I struggled for several years with this. Every time an invitation was given, I would grip the back of the pew in front of me so hard that I almost broke it in half.

Finally in 1979, we went on a youth choir mission trip as sponsors and I was so convicted of not "playing the game" any longer that when we got back from the tour, I made a profession of faith and followed in believer's baptism. I had for years been so worried about what people would think, let pride get in my way and let the devil convince me that I didn't need to give my life to Christ. What a peace came over me, once I turned loose of all of these things. Has everything been great since then? Of course not, but I do have open access to Jesus Christ as my Savior and He can comfort me, intercede for me, and be my best friend. I wouldn't trade that relationship for anything else in this world.

22. *Sharing question*: Write down any area of pride in your life that prevents you from being open and honest with those in the community of faith. What do you need to do about it?

Week Two: Adorned with Beauty through Trials

A Precious Word from God

> "And we know that all things to work together for good for those who love God, who are called according to his purpose, because those whom he foreknew, he also predestined to be conformed to the image of his Son, that his Son would be the firstborn among many brothers and sisters."
> Romans 8:28-29 (NET)

Introduction

The words of Romans 8:28-29 are some of my favorites in all the Scriptures for they help me understand that God is at work in all the events of my life to make me more like Jesus Christ. Although the circumstances themselves may not seem good, God uses them for my benefit to make me truly beautiful through the things that come my way. As we consider trials this week, think carefully about the beauty that God brings out of the ashes.

Day One Study

Reread 1 Peter 1:1-21 to see the flow of the passage and the context of what we will look at today.

1. According to v. 6, we greatly rejoice "in this." Go back through the 1:1-5 and list everything there in which you personally rejoice.

2. What do you learn about the nature of trials in v.6? In other words, what are they like according to this verse?

3. What is the final result of trials according to v. 7?

4. As you pray for believers who are experiencing trials, what can you pray for them according to vv. 6-7? Write down some specifics from these verses.

It helps me to see that the Bible says that trials can be distressing. So often as believers we think that living joyfully means that there is no distress. Joy is an inward attitude, but it doesn't rule out sorrow, pain, or grief. At times it helps me to turn to Scriptures such as this chapter in 1 Peter so that I am reminded of the reasons to be joyful. When I begin to get depressed over my circumstances, I need to refocus on Jesus and on His promises.

5. *Sharing question*: Are you in the midst of a trial that is distressing you? What is it? Be prepared to share it with your group so that they can pray for you.

6. *Sharing question*: Describe one way that you have found that helps you bring your focus back to God when you are in the midst of a trial.

- *Diamonds in the Word* -In the Psalms we often see the distress caused by trials as the psalmist opens his heart before the Lord. Read Psalm 13, 22 (Much of this psalm is prophetic about Jesus but consider David's feelings as he wrote these words), and 38. Write down what you learn about pouring out your heart before the Lord from David.

Day Two Study

Reread 1 Peter 1:6-7.

7. Verse 7 says that your faith may be tested by fire through trials. When you took tests in school, what was the purpose of the test? (Hint - It was not to get a grade!)

- *Diamonds in the Word* -Look up the Greek for tested (NAS & NKJV) or tried (KJV) in v. 7. Write down the definition.

In my education classes in college, I remember hearing that tests should also be teaching tools. The test itself can help the students learn. At the time I didn't really believe that it could be true, but I remember an exam at seminary where I went straight home and looked up the questions that I had skipped. I had somehow missed the information and actually wanted to learn about them!

8. *Sharing question*: Share with your group about a trial you have experienced that taught you while it tested your faith. Share what happened and what you learned as a result of that trial.

9. Response to God: Write a prayer to God asking Him to help you learn what He needs to teach you through a specific situation that you are facing right now. Ask him to make you a more beautiful woman from what you learn.

Day Three Study

Reread 1 Peter 1:6-21.

We saw in our Day One lesson that there are reasons to rejoice although we are dealing with trials in our lives. Peter talks about rejoicing later in this chapter.

10. What can help you rejoice according to 1:8-9?

We also saw in last week's lesson that we have been born again to a living hope (1:3). As Peter mentions trials, he also mentions hope. Sometimes we use the word hope to mean a possibility, a "hope" that something happens. That is not the idea of the hope here. The meaning of this hope is "Hope, desire of some good with expectation of obtaining it."[1] This kind of hope is one that you do expect to happen; it is not doubtful.

11. According to 1:13, 21, what truths can give us hope?

♦ *Diamonds in the Word* - Use your concordance to find other verses about hope. What do you learn from them that gives you hope?

12. *Sharing question*: Think of a difficult circumstance in your life right now. Perhaps you would call it a trial or perhaps just a difficult situation. How

---

[1] Spiros Zodhiates, *The Complete Word Study Dictionary: New Testament* (Chattanooga, TN: AMG Publishers, 1992), 570.

can the truths that you have learned here in 1 Peter about rejoicing and hope help you face this circumstance?

We do need to keep in mind that we are sometimes the cause of our own trials. We have sinned or just messed up and have created the consequences. Perhaps you are in deep debt because you have overspent, being enticed by materialism. You may have acted unwisely in dealing with other people and are left with problems in relationships. I know Christians who rarely consider their personal responsibility in their situations but tend to blame Satan for everything that happens to them. We will study our enemy more in the last lesson, but here we should understand that he is not all-powerful and that we are responsible for our choices and the consequences.

Yet, there is hope even when we have sinned and blown it!

Read Romans 8:18-30.

These verses can give us hope and reason to rejoice even when we have caused the problem ourselves. They teach us that God uses every situation to make us more beautiful because we become more like Christ.

13. Romans 8:28-29 is our "Precious Word from God" for this week. Copy it below and memorize at least v. 28.

14. *Sharing question*: Share with your group a time when you recognized the principles of Romans 8:28 as true, once you looked back on the situation.

15. Responding to God: Write a prayer thanking God for His redemption of your mistakes. Think of a specific time when you created a bad situation and yet, He brought good from it. Thank Him for the good He will bring from your current trial.

- *Diamonds in the Word* - What Bible story could you use to illustrate the truths of Rom. 8:28-29? Explain your choice.

Day Four Study

As we continue to consider the topic of trials in the life of a believer, we want to look at some other passages that may help us see them from God's perspective.

Read James 1:2-4, 12.

16. Explain the process and outcomes of trials that James describes.

17. What is your attitude to be in the midst of these trials? Why can you have this attitude according to James?

So often we hear the question, "How can a good God let this happen?" We need to remember in the midst of our trials that death, disease, and war entered the world because of the sin of mankind. Our lives involve pain and death because we are sinners. If you do not know the story of how sin entered this world, read Gen. 3.

Read John 9:1-3.

18. What was the purpose of the illness of this man that Jesus met?

The disciples believed that all illness was caused by specific sin in the person's life. We must never assume that any individual sickness or trial is because of that person's sin. That can be the case, but only God can reveal the reason for any trial, and we outsiders do not need to know. God gives us info only on a need to know basis☺ I don't need to know why you are experiencing a trial.

When I encounter a difficult circumstance, I take it before Lord for understanding. God does discipline us when we need it and we must be sensitive to what He is telling us in the midst of trials. It is hard to consider that we have sinned and that God is disciplining us for it. Our hearts are deceptive and we prefer to ignore our own sins or to minimize them.

19. List everything that you learn about God's discipline in Heb. 12:5-11.

20. *Sharing question*: Describe a time in your life when God disciplined you or when others attributed a trial in your life to your personal sins. How did you respond? How did it make you more beautiful?

- *Diamonds in the Word* - Use your concordance to look up discipline, especially in the book of Proverbs. What do you learn about disciplining children?

Day Five Study

What we learn from the verses we have seen this week is a larger perspective, the big picture, concerning trials in our lives. When we encounter difficult circumstances, God wants us to get a broader point-of-view than we can see from within the situation.

Reread 1 Peter 1:3-13; James 1:2-4, 12; Rom. 8:18-30; Heb. 12:5-13.

21. Summarize what you learn from all these passages about the larger perspective of our trials, i.e. what are some of God's purposes when believers face trials.

22. What truths have you learned from these passages about how to respond to trials?

These truths can help give us the hope and the joy that we are to have during hard times. However, often people need assistance to refocus on God and His goodness. I have learned to pray for God's wisdom in encouraging others because sometimes quoting Rom. 8:28 makes their sorrow or distress seem wrong or trivial. I have to be sensitive to their feelings in the words that I choose to bring comfort to them. We can have joy and sorrow at the same time, and we have to allow believers to deal with pain, which is not a sinful feeling.

23. *Sharing question*: What are some ways that other believers have helped you see the big picture when you have dealt with difficult times?

- *Diamonds in the Word* -What passages have helped you personally to make it through hard times?

Virginia's Story

The thing about difficult circumstances is that they are so... well, wearing! One or two - maybe even three difficulties at the same time can be dealt with, but when crisis upon crisis occurs like dominos falling, your body and mind do not have time to recover before the next crisis hits. The impact of stress on the body and mind leave you depleted of internal resources to cope, and you find yourself in despair. What can you do when you reach this level of physical, emotional, and spiritual weariness?

There was a time years ago when I found myself in this state. Loss of income, death of loved ones, shoulder surgery, loss of friendships and other disappointments had taken their toll on my mind and body. I felt I was so buried in despair I could never dig my way out. But I refused to give in to the pressure to give up and walk away from God. A few years prior to that time, I watched as people I knew and loved turned their back on God, and what they knew to be the right thing, in order to do what was right in their own eyes. I knew I did not want to do the same thing. Deep down, I knew that turning away from God was not the answer even though at times I felt forsaken.

When I sat down to pray, the words would not come. I found myself crying to God saying "O God, please do not let me go. Even though I have lost my grip on you, please do not let me go but keep me in the palm of your hand."

As I cried out to Him, I found Psalm 101:3. The words of this verse were like a surge of energy to my soul. "*I hate the work of those who fall away. It shall not fasten its grip on me*" (NASB)

This verse became my commitment to the Lord during a difficult time. My commitment was that I would not allow life's troubles to fasten their grip on me forcing me away from God and my faith. I felt I was losing my grip, but I also knew of God's promise to never leave me nor forsake me. I clung to that promise even during the times when I questioned it.

God heard the cry of a wounded heart, a defeated mind, and a weary body. He brought me out of the miry clay, set my feet upon the Rock, and filled my mouth with praise to My God. Psalm 40:1-3. He healed my broken heart, and has used the difficulties of my past to soften me in response to the pain of others. He has forced me, through my own suffering, to be more flexible, understanding, and patient when faced with the suffering of others. Broken relationships in my life have been mended because I am more forgiving having been taught forgiveness while in the fires of tribulation. I didn't like having to go through everything I went through, but God was with me through it all and has not wasted the experiences but is using them for His glory.

When trails come, it is so important to cling to what we know to be true from God's Word because His promises are true! The answer to the question in the first paragraph is "*fight back*". *Don't give up... don't give in, but fight back with Truth*!

- He will hear when you cry out to Him - Psalm 40:1
- He will comfort you - Isaiah 66:13
- He will be a refuge and source of strength to you - Psalm 46:1
- He will rescue you from despair - Psalm 42:11
- He will fill your heart with peace - Phil. 4:7
- He will fill your mouth with praise - Psalm 63:3

Thanks be to God that as I place my trust in Him no matter what life brings my way, I am blessed!

24. Response to God: Write a prayer in which you are completely honest with God about how you feel about a current trial or difficulty. Ask God to give you the grace to make it through whatever you are dealing with in your life right now. Ask Him to give you hope and joy in the midst of this situation.

25. Write a note to a friend who is struggling in her life to encourage her. Write a prayer for her that God will bring beauty within from the ashes.

Week Three: Adorned with Beauty through God's Word

A Precious Word from God

"The grass withers and the flower falls off,
but the word of the Lord endures forever."
1 Peter 1:24c-25 (NET)

Introduction

God's Word is our authority for life and godliness. It holds the truths that we are to believe and by which we are to live. My heart so wants you to believe what you read there and to open your life to all that God wants to do in you through His Word to make you a more beautiful woman. Just reading the Bible, however, is not enough - we must commit to live out what we see there; we must turn from the things that God hates and pursue the things that He loves; we must recognize that God is revealed in all that He does and seek Him in the stories of His Word and the truths that are stated about Him.

Day One Study

Read 1 Peter 1:22-2:3.

1. Write down all the commands or instructions that you are to do according to this passage. (You will recognize them by the lack of a subject. When I say to my child, "Clean your room," I do not put a subject as to who is to do it. The "you" is understood.)

2. Why would it be important to recognize the instructions given in a passage?

When you study a verse, it is helpful to consider how each phrase relates to the others. Every part of the verse will tell either who, what, where, when, how, or why about the main idea. This is one way to help us do the observation part of Bible study that forces us to really look carefully at what is being said. If you look for the answers to these kinds of questions as you read the Bible, you will be able to see amazing truths for yourself!

3. Here is 1 Peter 1:22 in the NASB: "Since you have in obedience to the truth purified your souls for a sincere love of the brethren, fervently love one another from the heart." Write down the phrases that answer these questions:

    a. What are they to do (the basic instruction)?

    b. How are they to do it (2 ways)?

    c. What have they already done that allows them to obey the instruction?

    d. Why are they to do this according to v. 23?

The truths that we are to obey are found in God's Word. God wants us to use the Scriptures like soap to scrub us clean of the things that make us dirty if we are to grow in beauty. I know that each day I need to be washed by God's soap. It reminds me of a shower when my hair and clothes are full of sand from being on the beach all day. There is no better feeling than to come out of there totally clean!

4. What does God promise about His cleansing power in 1 John 1:8-9?

5. Why is it necessary for you to be pure if you are to love others? What are some sins that might keep you from truly loving others?

♦ *Diamonds in the Word* -Read 1 Corinthians 13:1-8a. Look up the Greek words for the various qualities of love. How do you measure up with your husband, your roommate, your parents, or your boss?

Spend some time before God, asking Him to show you the areas of your life that are preventing you from truly loving other believers. You might even think of a specific person that you are having trouble loving (not a feeling but an action). Confess your lack of love and any sinful attitudes that God reveals to you.

6. *Sharing question*: What is one specific way that God has shown you to put 1 Peter 1:22 into action in your own life?

Day Two Study

Reread 1 Peter 1:22-25.

7. What do you learn about God's Word in these verses? Make a list of everything that is said about it. Use words straight out of the text. Don't paraphrase.

8. When we see a contrast between two things in the Scriptures, it makes an emphasis and helps us better understand God's point. How does the contrast in vv. 24-25 make Peter's point about God's Word stronger or help you understand it better?

This is your verse to memorize this week. How are you coming with your verses? It will help if you will review all of them each week. What were the verses from Week 1 and Week 2?

- *Diamonds in the Word* -Read Isaiah 40:1-11, which is where Peter gets his quote, and write down any additional insights that you have from the context of that passage about God's Word.

In 1:23 Peter says that God's Word is an agent in our salvation. In Wayne Grudem's commentary on 1 Peter, he says, "The implications for evangelism are obvious: ultimately it is neither our arguments nor our life example that will bring new life to an unbeliever, but the powerful words of God himself - words which we still have preserved today in Scriptures. It is in reading or hearing these words that people are given new life."[2]

9. How can we use the Scriptures when we share Christ with others without beating them over the head with the Bible? Share your ideas and/or strategies that have worked for you.

Reread 1 Peter 1:22-2:3.

The Bible uses many analogies to help us better understand truth. We are visual people and these images give us insights. We have already seen God's Word contrasted with the grass and flowers.

10. What other images are compared to the Scriptures in 1:23 and in 2:2? How do these two images help you in your understanding of the Bible? In other words, what truths do they show about the Word of God?

---

[2] Wayne Grudem, *1 Peter*, The Tyndale New Testament Commentaries, Leon Morris, ed. (Grand Rapids, MI: William B. Eerdmans Publishing Company, 2002), 91.

- *Diamonds in the Word* -What other images for God's Word are used in Scripture and where are they found? If you don't know of any, try using your concordance. How do they help you better understand the work of God's Word in our lives?

11. *Sharing question*: Describe a specific experience in your life when God's Word acted in ways like these images.

In order for the Scriptures to make a difference in our lives, we have to take it into our hearts. Although I would have always said that the Bible was important in my life, my actions would have proven otherwise. It's hard for God to speak to us when we aren't reading His Word, which is His message to men and women everywhere.

12. *Sharing question*: If the importance of God's Word to you were to be judged by the amount of time you spend in it, how would you be doing? Evaluate yourself on a scale of 1-5.

13. *Sharing question*: Think of a specific plan that you could implement in order to help you make the Word of God more of a priority. As your group shares these answers, you may get some good ideas from one another.

Day Three Study

Today we are going to take a short break from 1 Peter itself to study Psalm 119, which extols the benefits of God's Word in our lives. You may be aware that it is also the longest of all the Psalms. Don't worry; you don't have to read the whole thing unless you want to! Take your time as you read and truly think about the message that this Psalm has concerning the Scriptures.

- *Diamonds in the Word* -Read all of Psalm 119. Read the instructions to #14 below and write down the same kinds of insights for the entire Psalm. You will have to use a separate piece of paper for any that aren't listed below.

14. Read these verses from Psalm 119 and meditate upon both their significance in your personal life and also the benefits that God's Word can bring to us when we pay attention to it. Choose a favorite from the group and copy it at the bottom of the list. Write down your insights:

    a. vv. 1-2

    b. v. 11

c. v. 14

d. v. 24

e. v. 28

f. v. 38

g. v. 50

h. vv. 97-100

i. v. 103

j. v. 105

k. v. 165

My favorite verse from Psalm 119:

15. Responding to God: Several of the verses in this Psalm are prayers as the Psalmist asks God to take the Word and use it in a personal way in his life - vv. 18, 25, 58, 133, 169. Read these verses and then write a prayer, a song, a poem, or a psalm from your own heart incorporating the thoughts that you want to pray for yourself. You can draw a picture if you prefer. Use whatever meaningful method works best for you to respond to God!

16. *Sharing question*: Has there ever been a time in your life when God used His word in a similar way? Share with your group your praises about that situation.

Day Four Study

Today we return to 1 Peter as we continue to look at God's Word and its work in making us beautiful.

Reread 1 Peter 2:1-3.

17. In our Day One Study we looked at the instructions or commands in the passage from 1:22-2:3. One of them is found in 2:2. Copy it below:

18. We already noticed the analogy in 2:2 describing how we should relate to God's Word and why. How does this picture help you understand Peter's instruction?

19. Look again at 1 Peter 2:1. What is the prerequisite for growing in God's Word? Why would that be necessary if you are to grow more beautiful internally?

When Peter tells us to be like babies, he doesn't mean that in a bad way. Even if we are mature believers, we are to still act like babies in the sense that he suggests. In fact, by acting like a baby, we become mature. Some believers are like children who are stunted in their growth because they don't eat as they should. Doctors always check a baby's growth to make sure that she is growing in accordance with her age. I am glad that no one had a spiritual growth chart with which to compare me for much of my Christian life! What if there could be a way to measure our growth at church each week - sort of a check-up? How embarrassing to be a Christian for years and still look like a baby!

20. Compare similarities you see between immature believers and the actions of children. (No names and no specific stories!!!)

- *Diamonds in the Word* -Paul describes the Corinthians as "babes" (NKJV). Read 1 Corinthians 3:1-9. Sometimes we miss the fact that the "fleshly" (NASB) or "carnal" (NKJV) believers are synonymous with infants in Christ. What do you learn here (and in the rest of this book if you have time to read it) about the actions of Christians who are acting like babies?

21. *Sharing question*: Is your growth consistent with your age as a believer? Why or why not? Name one specific thing that you will do in applying 1 Peter 2:1-3. Write it in the first person - "I will . . . ."

Day Five Study

When we looked at Psalm 119 we saw that God's Word is a lamp to our feet and a light to our path in times of confusion; it is our counselor in times of uncertainty; it brings us peace in times of distress. I am sure that you can testify to periods in your own life when the Scriptures impacted you in those kinds of ways.

22. What does the Bible do for us according to Hebrews 4:12?

23. What do you learn in 2 Timothy 3:16 about the work of the Scriptures?

In the following story, Betty Jo shares how God's words from Habakkuk have been both a light and a peace in her life. Look up Habakkuk 2:2-4 and 3:17-19 before you read her story.

Betty Jo's Story

Beginning in December 2000, the words in Habakkuk 2:2-4; 3:17-19 took on personal meaning for my husband and me. After twenty-four years on staff in a sports ministry, my husband and I felt the Lord telling us to take a huge step of faith and walk away from it--to come aside for a sabbatical season with the Lord while awaiting His next assignment. Little did we know at that time that His timing would be much longer than anything we could have imagined.

We began to "watch" intently as several opportunities were presented, but kept being impressed that we were to continue to "wait." One day about six weeks after our resignation, I remember my husband (being very much the male and Type A personality) declaring that we had "waited" long enough and surely the sabbatical season was over. It was time for him to get a job and move on with the next assignment, a new "passion", as many well-meaning friends encouraged him to find. About three months after this declaration, during his morning quiet time, the Lord spoke to his heart: "Dennis, You keep looking for your new passion. You said you had passion for coaching and then for ministry, but now you are struggling with finding a new passion. The reason you can't find a new passion is because I never intended for you to have a passion for anything but ME! All of your passion is to be attached to ME, not another job. Be patient, I will give you another assignment. But right now, you are to concentrate on sitting at MY feet and being more like Mary and less like Martha." So the waiting continued. About eighteen months later, God began to give the "vision" and we began "to write it down". Currently we are still in the process of "writing it down" (almost two and half years after He gave us the verses in Habakkuk 2:2-4). It has been a definite re-shaping of my husband's posture and position before the Lord.

Habakkuk 3:17-19 has been such a comfort during this time when material things appear so barren. Each time that we turn on the news or read a paper declaring the drastic decline of the economy and record unemployment increases, or hear reports of long-time established ministries financially struggling, only God's assurances in His Sovereign plan keep us going forward. Attendance at any peer function usually includes being asked, "What are you doing now?"; once again, these verses sustain us. As our savings account is now depleted and our meager ministry retirement fund dwindles, we are "rejoicing in the Lord and being joyful in God our Savior." The Sovereign Lord is (has been and will continue to be) our strength.

Our prayer has been always to know Him better, deeper, and to go to new heights with Him. We have now come to realize that passion for Him does not mean the absence of wilderness experiences in our soul along the journey. But rather passion is a Spirit-led ability to walk in obedience--bringing deep joy to the soul--even when His answers to our prayers don't come wrapped like we expect. However, we are grateful for His wrappings today, because He has shown us what true passion for Him means: to trust Him when our eyes cannot see and our minds cannot perceive, knowing that He walks beside us to take us to the heights. In these past two and a half years, our intimacy with Him has grown sweeter, richer and fuller than ever before. "But thanks be to God! He gives us the victory through our Lord Jesus Christ." (I Cor. 15:57)

In various situations of life we turn to various verses as our strength. I like to have them memorized, but if not, I find it helpful to write them down where they are handy as I pray. In times of trouble, I have often turned to the Psalms for strength or reassurance. In grief, there is comfort in God's promises of heaven. As I pray for what looks hopeless, I remember that nothing is impossible for God to do (Jer. 32:17). When I pray for my children, I often ask Him to complete the good work that He has begun in them (Phil. 1:6). Many of you probably have favorite verses that you use as you pray for certain things. There is power in the Word of God and it is so helpful to pray that word back to Him. Then we know that we are praying with the mind of Christ and in His will.

- *Diamonds in the Word* -Find some verses that you can claim in a specific situation in your life right now by using your concordance. Write them on cards or put them in a journal that you can carry with you and whip out whenever you need a reminder of God's power and His promises for specific situations.

24. *Sharing question*: We have seen this week that one of the ways that we are adorned with true beauty is through the power of God's Word. Share a way that God has used the Bible in your life to make you more beautiful.

25. Responding to God: Write a prayer thanking God for the power, comfort, etc. of His Word. Incorporate some of the verses that have been meaningful to you this week as you write.

Week Four: Adorned with the Beauty of Holiness

A Precious Word from God

> "But you are a chosen race, a royal priesthood, a holy nation, a people of his own, so that you may proclaim the virtues of the one who called you out of darkness into his marvelous light."
> 1 Peter 2:9 (NET)

Introduction

So far in our study of 1 Peter, we have focused on the beauty that comes from faith, from trials and from God's Word. This week we will look at holiness and the beauty that comes into our lives as we seek to have a lifestyle that honors the God who called us to be His and to be holy. I hope that you are able to work daily on these lessons and allow God to speak to you personally. I know that when I rush through questions just to get answers, I am not allowing God to do His work in me, to use His Word in a powerful way as we saw last week. Before you begin reading and answering questions, take the time to quiet your heart before God and ask Him to speak to you in a very personal and practical way as you open His Word.

Day One Study

Read 1 Peter 1:13-2:10.

We are going to backtrack just a bit today into Chapter 1. You have read it several times already. It is a rich chapter, full of so many wonderful truths that we can't cover them all in depth, despite all the homework I am giving you☺ Today we are going to focus on 1:13-21. They will relate to some verses in Chapter Two that we will pick up later this week.

1. There are a number of instructions given in 1:13-21. List them just as they are written. Some of them are accompanied by phrases that tell us "why" we are to obey them. If you see any of those, list them with the instruction, beginning it with the question "why?" I have given you the first one.

1. Prepare your minds for action   Why? (Therefore refers back to vv. 10-12)

Because of our great salvation about which the prophets & angels wondered

- *Diamonds in the Word*--Using your Greek tools, look up the key words in the instructions and write out more detailed versions of the verses you just listed.

These instructions involve some specific actions that we are to take as believers. It is so easy to just read them quickly and dismiss them by thinking, "Oh, I do that." But do we really do what we are instructed to do here? I have to admit that I come up short. For one thing, I am not completely focused on my ultimate salvation. I am way too distracted by the here and the now.

2. *Sharing question*: Go back through your list of instructions and meditate upon each one. Consider whether you are really obeying them. Are you really preparing your mind for action? What would that look like? Write down your responses to each one.

3. There seems to be a contrast in vv. 14-15 in the instructions. We are told not to do one thing but instead to do the other. How does this help you better understand what holiness involves?

The words holy and sanctified are the same in the Greek, which means separated or set apart. When used of God, holiness reflects His essential character, which is separate from that of people. When used of believers, it involves "a sense of belonging to God, a people marked off and separate from the world by their way of life."[3]

---

[3] I. Howard Marshall, *1 Peter*, The IVP New Testament Commentary Series, Grant R. Osborne, ed. (Downers Grove, IL: InterVarsity Press, 1991), 53.

- *Diamonds in the Word*--Look up the words "holy" and "sanctify" (in all forms of the words) in your concordance. Look up every verse where they are used in 1 Peter. Write down your thoughts as you consider Peter's message to you about holiness.

4. *Sharing question*: Do people know that you are a Christian by your lifestyle? Are you any different from anyone else? I am not suggesting a holier-than-thou attitude where you are known more for what you don't do than for your love and godliness. Spend some time evaluating your attitudes as well as your actions. How godly are they? Share one area in your life where you need God to change you to be more like Him.

5. Responding to God: Respond to God with a prayer, poem, etc. Confess the ungodliness you see, the area where you are not holy as He is holy. Thank Him for the cleansing He gives through the washing of His Word and the conviction of His Spirit.

Day Two Study

Read 1 Peter 2:4-10.

6. In vv. 4-8 Peter uses the analogy of a stone for Jesus. List the various adjectives or phrases that he uses to describe this Stone. I have given you the first example.

    Living

7. Look up in the notes in your study Bible, or even in a regular English dictionary, and write down what you learn about cornerstones.

♦ *Diamonds in the Word*: Look up the cross references given in your Bible to 1 Peter 2:4-8. Peter quotes here extensively from the Old Testament. What do you learn from the context of the original passages?

Peter uses the Old Testament to make his points in chapter 2. In 1 Peter 2:7 he quotes Psalm 118:22. Jesus applied Psalm 118:22 to Himself in Matthew 21:33-46. Read the verses in Matthew.

8. Who does Jesus indicate has rejected Him? Why would they be similar to builders? How does the parable relate to Jesus' being a rejected stone?

9. *Sharing question*: Describe a time when your friends or those whom you were trying to help rejected you. Describe your feelings.

10. Explain how the metaphor of the stone enables you to understand more about Jesus. Write down personal insights from your list of adjectives in #6.

11. Responding to God: Are you among those who disbelieve and reject the Stone, stumbling over Him? Or is Jesus a Stone of precious value for you? Write a letter or a prayer to Jesus. Tell Him how valuable He is in your life.

Day Three Study

Reread 1 Peter 2:1-10.

12. List all the descriptions that Peter uses for believers in vv. 5-10.

13. *Sharing question*: Which one of these descriptions is most meaningful to you? Why?

It is a major truth in the New Testament that the Gentiles were once not part of God's people but in Jesus Christ, they are. In the Old Testament it was only the Jews who were God's people; they were His holy nation, set apart for Him. **Read Ephesians 2:11-22**.

14. What metaphors does Paul use here that we also see 1 Peter 2?

15. Are there any barriers left between the Jews and the Gentiles when we believe in Christ? Support your conclusion from this passage.

16. What privileges does Paul mention that we have as God's children?

17. *Sharing question*: What do these privileges mean to you personally and why?

The Jews were given wonderful privileges in the Old Covenant, which came to them under Moses. However, they began to believe that they were better than other nations. They had God's favor and it went to their heads. Rather than living gratefully, knowing that it was only by the mercy of God that they were brought into His family, they began to think they deserved His favor. You can see this particularly in the lives of the Pharisees.

- *Diamonds in the Word*--Find an incident in the life of Christ where Jesus deals with the Pharisees who are being self-righteous. What do you learn about being self-righteous from Jesus' interactions with them?

Do you ever begin to believe that you have somehow deserved the mercy of God because you are so holy? Do you begin to look around you at the world and think that you are so much better than everyone else? It's easy in our culture to look pretty good compared to someone else. However, it is a lie. We are what we are solely because of God's grace, which we don't deserve. It is only His work in us that makes us holy, not because we have done it ourselves.

18. Responding to God: Write a response to God concerning any self-righteousness that you see in your life.

Day Four Study

In both 1 Peter 2:5 and 2:9 believers are called a priesthood. You may have heard of the doctrine of "the priesthood of the believer." Today we are going to look at what it means to be a priest before our God.

Dr. D. Edmond Hiebert explains the priesthood of the believer: "Since all believers constitute a priesthood, there is no longer any place for a special office of priests to mediate between individual believers and God; each believer has direct access to God Himself."[4] This is why in our Protestant churches our leaders are not priests but ministers and pastors and why we do not go to them for confession but directly before God Himself.

19. Read 1 Tim. 2:5. Why do we no longer need someone else, a priest, to go to God on our behalf?

20. Read Heb. 4:14-16. What do you learn here about our situation in prayer as believers in Jesus.

- *Diamonds in the Word*--Research Old Testament priests in a Bible dictionary or encyclopedia. What do you learn about their qualifications and their job descriptions? Do you see any application for us as God's priests today?

---

[4] D. Edmond Hiebert, *First Peter: An Expositional Commentary* (Chicago, IL: Moody Press, 1984), 123-124.

21. Read these verses and identify the kinds of spiritual sacrifices we make as priests:

    a. Psalm 107:22

    b. Psalm 141:2

    c. Phil 4:18

    d. Rom. 12:1

    e. Heb. 13:15

    f. Rom. 15:16

22. *Sharing question*: Look back over your list of spiritual sacrifices. As a priest, are you presenting these kinds of sacrifices to God consistently? Write down one area where you can improve and a specific action you can take this week in that area.

- *Diamonds in the Word*: Paul describes himself as a drink offering in both Phil. 2:17 and 2 Tim. 4:6. Read those verses. Look in your concordance for drink offering in the Old Testament to find out what it was. What insights do you learn about Paul from the drink offering? How can you be a drink offering in your own life?

23. Responding to God: Respond to God in any way you like - a prayer, a poem, a drawing, or a song. Tell Him what it means to you to be able to come directly before His throne of grace without needing anyone else except Jesus. Keep in mind that as a priest, you are to be holy as you come before Him.

Day Five Study

Our "Precious Word from God" this week is 1 Peter 2:9. Reread it.

24. The first part of this verse deals with our identity and lifestyle. What does a holy life enable us to do according to the end of the verse? Are they necessarily related? Why or why not?

25. If you were to proclaim God's excellencies, what would you say?

26. Copy this verse below and work on memorizing it.

For this lesson I received two really good stories about how a woman's lifestyle was a witness to Christ. Rather than choosing one, I am going to let you read them both.

Kathy's Story

When our children were young we had our next-door neighbor's teenage daughter baby-sit for us from time to time. She was a sweet young girl and we enjoyed having her in our home whenever she wanted to come over. One day she asked me "Why is your family so different? You all don't argue and fuss and you seem to have such love for each other." I told her that we loved the Lord and that He is the one that made the difference in our home. It was His love that she saw and was drawn to. We talked and I shared Christ with her but she didn't seem to really understand what I was telling her.

She went off to Baylor for college and one of the first times she was home she came over and said. "Now I know what you were trying to tell me. You all have a personal relationship with God through Christ." She had become a Christian and was so excited to share her new faith with us. I am thankful for the seeds that were sown in her life and for the ultimate new life in Christ that she was given.

Julia's Story

I met a wonderful young mom, and we quickly became friends. We talked on the phone and occasionally got together since we had kids the same age. I also gave her kids Bible related gifts for their birthdays - Veggie Tales videos and kids sing-a-long Praises tapes. This was one of those "intentional relationships" that our pastor encourages us to cultivate with others. We had conversations about church, but I could tell that she did not have a personal relationship with Christ. She did not rely on Him to direct her daily decisions, and I'm not sure she even owned a Bible.

One day, she called me crying and said she just caught her husband in an affair that had been going on for a year. Once the affair was in the open, he had a decision to make. Did he want his marriage and his children, or did he want this other woman? He was convinced he was in love with this other woman, and he wasn't sure if he wanted to make his marriage work. She desperately wanted to keep her marriage together but wasn't sure that she could move past this hurt.

I invited her to my home so I could visit with her. We sat on my couch, and she poured her heart out. God gave me the ability to listen, and He also gave me the words to soothe her. She looked at me and said, "I want what you have." I think I've waited my whole life to hear those words. I knew my life was different, but didn't realize that others saw it! She recognized that God was in control of my life, and I had Him to lean on in times of crisis. I had witnessed to her by my lifestyle. I was able to tell her what was missing from her life by clearly sharing the gospel. She didn't pray to receive Christ at that moment, but I gave her a Bible, hugged her, and prayed with her.

God urged me to call her husband and visit with him after she left. I really didn't know him that well, but when I called him, I was not judgmental. I knew that he was having a hard time, too. Since he was waffling between staying and leaving, I encouraged him to stay. He said the marriage was dead - that they had no marriage at all - that they were just friends. I told him that that was something! I asked about his kids and if he was willing to give them up. He said he couldn't stay together just for the kids - that that wouldn't be any life for any of them. I told him that God could make it work. If he stayed now even if just for the kids, God could put this back together. I told him that if Christ became the center of their marriage, it wouldn't fail. He asked me if God hated him. I told him no - he hates the sin, but not you. I also reminded him how wonderful his wife was and that he was crazy to consider anyone else. Life with this other girl wouldn't always feel this way. I told him that he was in the early stages of "love" and that those feelings would go away with her, too. Marriage is a choice and it has to be worked on. We ended the conversation, and he still didn't know what he wanted.

She left town for one week with her kids. I sent her a card every day explaining why she was wonderful. (She felt like she wasn't because her husband didn't want her.) She took her Bible with her. She later told me that she read it every day and that she decided to let the Lord lead her life!

The whole time she was gone I prayed that her husband would miss them. He had a choice: he could have gone to be with that other woman, but he didn't. He stayed at home, alone, missing his family. Before the week was up, he drove to get her.

This was far from over because my friend had entered another phase of the grieving cycle. Now she was angry. She came home with him, but wasn't sure she was going to be able to forgive him. And, with all of the fighting, he wasn't sure this was going to work out - other woman or not. I had run out of things to say and knew I was in over my head. She went with me to talk with one of our ministers. The minister asked her if she was willing to serve her husband - regardless of how he treated her. She decided at that moment that God was calling her to stay in her marriage, forgive her husband and serve him!

She went home and served her husband. That made such a difference. She read her Bible; she started listening to Christian radio stations; and she served him. He has said that her attitude toward him, even though he wasn't treating her nicely, is what ultimately made him stay. What a witness she was to him!

They attend church regularly at a Bible teaching church, so seeds are being planted if not cultivated and growing. Their marriage is better today than it ever has been. I love seeing them together! They are so happy. They worked out some underlying issues in their marriage that they didn't realize needed to be worked on. Praise the Lord. He put me in the right place at the right time and gave me the opportunity to witness through my lifestyle. This is an experience that I'll never forget.

You can see that others were able to see the beauty of the Lord in the lives of these women, and that beauty was an attraction. Those who didn't know Christ asked about the difference for they recognized something beautiful. As we grow in holiness, we become more beautiful because we are more like Jesus.

27. *Sharing question*: Share a story from your own life in which your lifestyle impacted someone else in a similar way.

Week Five: Adorned with Beauty among Unbelievers

A Precious Word from God

"Maintain good conduct among the non-Christians"
1 Peter 2:12a

Introduction

Beauty attracts attention. You can see this in a crowded place when a beautiful woman enters. The groups in museums encircle the loveliest pieces of art. Cars stop by the side of a road so the passengers can watch a magnificent sunset. We want to surround ourselves with beautiful things. If we are to attract those who are looking for a faith that is real, we will do so only when we show forth an inner beauty that draws others to the Savior.

Day One Study

Read 1 Peter 2:11-3:7 to get the flow of the entire passage.

1. The first two verses of this passage (2:11-12) basically sum up the overall teaching of this section of the book. What two principles are you to follow according to these verses? What result does Peter hope will come from your obedience (v.12)? Memorize v. 12a, our verse for the week.

2. Why do you think that Peter would remind his readers that we are strangers and aliens in this world at this point in the letter?

The term "fleshly desires" (NET) or "fleshly lusts" (NASB) sounds like these must be sexual acts of some kind. Dr. D. Edmond Hiebert explains this: "Peter's words should not be interpreted to mean that desires related to our physical nature are evil, as though the human body in itself was evil. The thought is not limited to sensual indulgences; Peter's words circumscribe all those cravings associated with the entire nature of man as a fallen being, whether they express themselves through the body or the mind. Flesh is used in its ethical sense to denote fallen mankind as characterized by depraved and corrupting desires."[5]

3. Read these cross references and write down your insights about fleshly desires:

    a. Galatians 5:19-21

    b. Ephesians 5:3-5

    c. 1 John 2:15-17

---

[5] Hiebert, 144.

4. We are prone to think about fleshly desires as "Top Ten" sins. What do you see in these verses that proves that not to be true? How can these "minor" sins make us less than beautiful?

5. *Sharing question*: What deeds or attitudes of the flesh convict you personally from this list and why?

- *Diamonds in the Word*: Illustrate the truth that "fleshly desires that do battle against the soul" with a story from the Scriptures.

6. Responding to God: Write down what is on your heart as God has used these Scriptures to speak to you today. Again, use whatever means works for you - a letter, a poem, a song or a prayer.

Day Two Study

Reread 1 Peter 2:11-17.

7. List the things we are to do according to 2:13-17. Also write beside them "why" the verses indicate we are to do them. In other words, what does God want to achieve by our doing these things? How does God's purpose relate back to 2:11-12?

♦ *Diamonds in the Word*: Look up the Greek word for bondslaves (NASB) in v. 16. Cross-reference this word and write down all that you learn about what it means to be a bondslave of God.

8. Compare 2:13-17 with Romans 13:1-7. Write down similarities as well as additional insights from the Romans passage.

God's purposes for our submission to government show us that we are obedient to the law when it means doing what is right. It glorifies God and makes us beautiful in the eyes of others to do the right thing. We have little witness before unbelievers when we break the law. I served on the grand jury, a real eye-opener! It was heart-breaking to be faced with the indictment of those who claimed to be Christians but who had lost their witness.

9. *Sharing question*: Review the instructions you listed in #7. How does it look to honor someone? Maybe you like the current President and find him easy to honor, but do you honor every President despite his political perspective? How do you honor other people in specific ways?

10. Responding to God: Read 1 Timothy 2:1-4. Write a prayer for our President and some of our other governmental leaders, keeping in mind the reasons Paul calls us to pray for them.

1 Peter 2:11-3:7 mentions submission several times. Dr. Spiros Zodhiates helps us understand the Greek word submit, *hupotasso*. It is a compound word meaning "to place in order"[6] that comes from the root word *hupo*, meaning under or beneath[7], and *tasso*, "to place, set, appoint, arrange, order"[8]. In these verses,

---

[6] *Complete Word Study Dictionary*, 1427.

[7] *Complete Word Study Dictionary*, 1419.

[8] *Complete Word Study Dictionary*, 1367.

it is in the middle voice in the Greek, meaning to place oneself in submission. Thus, literally it means to put yourself beneath someone. It is used in the military, meaning, "to place under rank."[9]

If you are like me, you feel that you are a good, obedient citizen if you haven't been convicted of any felonies lately. However, there is more to this than merely criminal laws.

11. What are some ways that you see Americans fail to submit to the law and consider it no big deal? *Sharing question*: In what area(s) have you been guilty?

Day Three Study

There are limits to submission, and the Scriptural example helps us understand when to draw the line and say no. We'll read a story in Acts to help us understand the principle and then return to 1 Peter.

Read Acts 3:1-4:31.

[9] Warren W. Wiersbe, *Be Hopeful* (Wheaton, IL: Victor Books, 1984), 68.

12. Summarize Peter and John's story and how the governmental authorities responded.

13. What do you learn from Peter and John's example about the limits of submission to governmental authorities? Explain the limits as you would to someone questioning you about it.

Reread 1 Peter 2:13-3:7.

14. What phrases in this passage support Peter and John's refusal to submit in the Acts story? Explain how they support limits on submission.

Read Daniel 1:1-21.

15. What do you learn from Daniel about how to honor those in authority when you encounter a situation where you cannot submit?

- *Diamonds in the Word*: Read Daniel 3:1-30 and 6:1-28, also. What do you see in these stories that relates to submission and government and the limits of submission?

16. *Sharing question*: Write the story of a situation where you failed to submit and suffered consequences. It may be a time when you were wrong not to submit or when you were justified in not submitting.

Day Four Study

Reread 1 Peter 2:11-25.

17. What kinds of masters are slaves to obey? Why?

18. Consider this passage in light of 2:12. What is God's overall purpose in calling slaves to submit?

We are thankful that we no longer have slavery in the United States; however, there are many parts of the world where there are slaves, although this fact is somewhat hidden in the cultures where slavery is practiced. I am grateful for Christians such as William Wilberforce and Harriet Beecher Stowe, the author of *Uncle Tom's Cabin*, whose actions led to the outlawing of slavery in Britain and the United States. They realized that although God called slaves to submit because He had a higher purpose, this institution did not reflect the character of God and needed outlawing. Their godly compassion led them to speak out.

So how does this passage apply to us today? There is not a direct correlation between slavery and employment. It is not the same in any way. Employees have freedom and opportunity to speak out that slaves never had. Yet, I think there is an attitude involved that we need to apply from this passage.

19. What do you learn from Jesus' example in 1 Peter 2:21-25 about attitude in the midst of mistreatment? Consider what His concern was when He went to the cross. How does it parallel the concern of this whole section of the book as expressed in 2:12?

- *Diamonds in the Word*: Read the gospel accounts of Jesus' trials and crucifixion. What do you learn from Him about keeping God's higher purpose in mind and bearing up under injustice?

God is not necessarily asking us to suffer unjustly in our workplace and keep quiet about it; yet, we must have the right attitude as Jesus did and we must consider God's higher purpose of 2:12. Too often we have mistakenly believed that Christians are not supposed to speak out about injustice and mistreatment, having somewhat

of a martyr complex. God is concerned about injustice and unrighteousness more than we are because He is just and righteous in all His ways. As we pray about how to handle such situations, we take all of this into account.

20. *Sharing question*: Do you evidence Jesus' attitude in your workplace? How would your fellow employees see this in your life?

21. *Sharing question*: What is one way that works for you to help you keep the right attitude when you are faced with difficult or foolish people?

22. Responding to God: It can be extremely difficult to work for unreasonable, unjust, or unwise people. If you are employed outside of the home, write a prayer concerning your own attitude at work. Pray for your supervisor as well. If you work for a fair and caring boss, write a prayer of thanks. If you are not employed, write a letter of encouragement to a friend who is. Pray for her every day this week.

Day Five Study

It is difficult to submit to an authority who is foolish, misguided, unwise, or just mistaken. You may work under the supervision of someone who makes bad choices for that business. Yet, there is nothing really wrong in what he asks you to do; thus, you must submit. You may disagree with the tax laws because the money is spent foolishly; yet, you must submit and pay your share. What is the key to submitting when you see such situations? I believe it is faith. Do you trust God to handle the situation? Do you believe that God is at work in whatever happens? Do you believe that Romans 8:28 is really true and that God will use this to make you more beautiful within? Do you believe that God will use your right actions and attitude to be a witness to those around you?

- *Diamonds in the Word*: Explain what you have learned about submission to government and bosses in a way that you could share with a new believer. How would you approach a situation at work when asked to do something suspect?

The bottom line of this lesson is being a light in the darkness, living with excellence before a world that doesn't know Jesus. People notice when we fail to live up to what we profess to believe. What kind of witness are you in your everyday life? Does your excellence at work reflect the God of excellence? Does your witness extend to the words that you say about people? In what areas do you need to work on excellence?

This story is from my own experience. I had hoped to receive one that I could use from a friend, but since I never did, I will share something from my own life about having excellent behavior among those who do not believe. I am sorry to say it is a story about what not to do!

Kay's Story

As I look back on my life, I am so ashamed of the wasted years when I didn't openly live for Christ. No one would have accused me of being a Christian for there was no evidence that I was. I certainly did not behave with excellence according to God's standards. If I had suggested that I was a Christian in those years, I would surely have been called a hypocrite!

My concern at that point in my life was to be accepted and fit in. It is so humiliating to realize that there are some people whom I knew then that would still have a hard time accepting that I am a believer. I talked about others behind their backs; I used bad language; I laughed at dirty jokes; I went to places where I should not have been and avoided church like a plague. I cannot remember being particularly kind to anyone and certainly had little love for anyone who didn't love me first.

How do I live with the fact that I was an embarrassment to Jesus? How do I go on and actually serve God when I brought Him shame before unbelievers? I can do that because I trust that He will use even my sins and mistakes for His glory and for my good. I live with the daily belief that He is more powerful than my sins. I accept His grace and His forgiveness and really believe that He gives more grace than I could ever need. I take it to heart that He is using even that period when I didn't walk with Him to make me more like Jesus. I recite Romans 8:28: "And we know that God causes all things to work together for good to those who love God, to those who are called according to His purpose. For those whom He foreknew, He also predestined to become conformed to the image of His Son, so that He would be the firstborn among many brethren."

God has surely used that time in my life to help me recognize His amazing grace for me, a sinner. He has helped me learn to give grace to those who are faltering because I was once there. I have seen His mercy and love and know that I am only here because of it. I am grateful that He can redeem even what is dark and ugly and make me more beautiful because of it.

23. *Sharing question*: What has God said to you this week?

Week Six: Adorned with the Beauty of a Gentle and Quiet Spirit

A Precious Word from God

"Let your beauty not be external - the braiding of hair and wearing of gold jewelry or fine clothes - but the inner person of the heart, the lasting beauty of a gentle and tranquil spirit, which is precious in the God's sight."
1 Peter 3:3-4 (NET)

Introduction

The verses that we have to memorize are those from which I took the title of this study. The word for beauty could be translated adornment. Although the words are found in this particular context, the thought that our primary adornment is to be in the heart applies to every area of our lives as women of God. Memorize these verses to help you remember what true beauty is all about.

Some of this lesson will be about marriage, and I realize that not all of you are married; however, we all do need to learn to have gentle and tranquil spirits. If you are single, there will be applications for you. Certainly, we all need to know what God says rather than what the world says about marriage so that we are prepared to stand for truth in a time of relativity. God designed marriage, and it is generally best to refer to the manufacturer's instructions if we want it to work.

Day One Study

Reread 1 Peter 3:1-7.

1. Does 1 Peter 3:3 that mean that women should not wear gold rings, etc.? Carefully read the verse and any notes in your Bible, and explain your reasoning.

2. Peter describes the gentle and tranquil (quiet in NASB) spirit and its importance in v. 4. What descriptive phrases or adjectives are used and how do they emphasize the need for this kind of spirit? How does this help us understand that this is for all women, not just wives?

The idea of a gentle and quiet spirit used to really bother me. I am not particularly quiet spoken. When I get excited, sometimes my husband reminds me to speak more softly. When I really looked at these verses, I realized that it doesn't say a gentle and quiet voice. How exciting! But what does it mean, then, to have a gentle and tranquil spirit? Dr. Wayne Grudem says that gentle means "'not insistent on one's own rights' or 'not pushy,' 'not selfishly assertive, not demanding one's own way.'"[10]

3. Look up these other verses that mention gentle or gentleness. Write down your thoughts and insights:

---

[10] Grudem, 140.

a. Matthew 5:5

b. Matthew 11:29

c. Galatians 5:22-23

4. *Sharing question*: In light of the verses on gentleness, what can you do to develop a more gentle and tranquil spirit?

♦ *Diamonds in the Word*: Considering the definition of gentle, give some examples from the life of Jesus where you see this quality in His life.

5. Responding to God: Confess to God your lack of showing a gentle and tranquil spirit (I expect that we all fall short in this). Ask Him to help you in this area.

Day Two Study

Reread 1 Peter 2:11-3:7.

6. How does Peter describe the kinds of husbands for whom he is concerned in 3:1? How does that relate to the general overriding purpose of God for our behavior in all these relationships according to 2:12?

In that day, the wife was expected to follow the religion of her husband. However, as the gospel spread, women came to faith in Jesus apart from their husbands, creating problems in the home. Although in our culture we are not expected to adopt the religion of our husbands, we have the same concern as these women in the first century that our husbands come to faith in Jesus.

7. What does Peter tell wives to do if they are to influence their husbands to faith?

8. If you are married, how can you apply these principles to issues other than salvation? If you are not married, are there situations where you can apply this?

9. *Sharing question*: Relate a story from your own life where you were influenced more by a person's actions and attitudes than her words.

- *Diamonds in the Word*: Read several commentaries or notes on this passage. What insights do you gain?

10. *Sharing question*: How are you doing in this area? Are you spending more time adorning your spirit or your body? Responding to God: Write a prayer being totally honest before God about your feelings and thoughts toward your husband or another person with whom you relate daily. Ask for God's help where you are struggling.

Day Three Study

Today we need to go back to the actual submission issue. As I mentioned in last week's lesson, there is much confusion about it. Some women see it as simply obeying whatever their husbands request without comment. I don't think that is the Scriptural principle for marriage at all. So to understand what it means to submit in marriage, we need to look at the major marriage principles back in the beginning, remembering that marriage was created by God in the garden before sin entered the world.

Read Genesis 2:18-25.

11. According to v. 18 God made woman as a helper. If you are to help your husband, does that mean silently standing by while he makes decisions? Why or why not?

12. Consider vv. 23-24. What is emphasized about the relationship of husband and wife? (You can find emphasis by the repetition of an idea, not necessarily the same wording.) If that is the way God describes marriage, what does that imply about decision-making?

Read Genesis 2:9-12.

13. What do you learn about submission in marriage, the wife/husband relationship, and God's will from this passage?

I believe that we are to submit to the leadership of our husbands as wives, but I also recognize that many have distorted what that means. I once read a book that made the command to submit into a higher law than the other commands of Scripture. It suggested that wives were to submit to any request and just trust God to protect them. Somehow the author denied our personal responsibility before God in obeying the other instructions of the Bible. Choosing to submit does not mean choosing sin. When it is blatantly sinful to submit, we must choose to obey the more specific instruction in God's Word.

In my marriage, submission rarely comes up because we work together in unity to make our decisions. When we do disagree, I have learned to defer to my husband who is responsible before God for the decision; however, I am responsible to share my perspective with him because I am his helper. Again, the key to my attitude is faith. I believe that God is powerful enough to change Gary's mind if He desires and can use a bad decision for our good; thus, God may choose to allow him to make a poor choice. Whatever consequences follow, our mighty God will use it in some way, even if the purpose is hidden from me. Because I believe that, I don't have to manipulate, pressure, or argue when I think I am right. I can respect my husband and know that it is between him and God. I state my perspective and then leave it between them. (I do have to add that I really have to pray through that sometimes, especially with money decisions☺)

14. Review Lesson Five, Day Three where we studied the limits on submission. Think of an example of a situation when a wife should not submit to her husband.

♦ *Diamonds in the Word*: Read Exodus 1:8-21. In light of the principles for submission from last week and this week's lessons, evaluate the response of the Hebrew midwives.

15. *Sharing question*: What is your attitude toward your husband's leadership? How can your group pray for you concerning this issue?

Day Four Study

Read the story of Abigail in 1 Samuel 25:2-42.

Abigail had a truly difficult husband and in this particular case, she chose to act in opposition to his decision concerning the matter of David and his men. She did not submit to his stated desires.

16. What benefits happened as a result of Abigail's actions, not only to her and her husband but also to David?

17. How do you see Abigail respect and honor Nabal even when she did not submit to him?

18. What lessons do you see in Abigail's life which apply to a difficult marriage and to submission?

Submission does not mean that you are to submit to physical abuse from your husband. When you are in danger of harm, you need to act wisely to protect yourself and your family. Although Abigail was not in physical danger from Nabal, both she and her husband were in danger, and she acted to protect them and their servants.

Peter uses Sarah as his example of a submissive wife in 3:5-6. He is probably not commenting on any specific action of Sarah's but on her general attitude and submissive heart. I have read some who use Sarah to suggest that we submit to anything that our husbands ask, but I don't think that is Peter's point here.

19. What does Peter emphasize about Sarah in 1 Peter 3:5-6?

- *Diamonds in the Word*: Study the life of Sarah from Genesis 12-23, and comment on what you learn from her about submission. Why do you think that God chose her to be the example for us of our attitudes toward our husbands? Think through the stories in Gen. 12:10-20; 20:1-18, and how they relate to the limits of submission that we studied last week. Was Sarah right to submit?

Again, attitude has a lot to do with submission. I find that when I respect my husband and expect him to make good decisions that he never has a problem with my sharing my opinions as well (and may decide that I am right); however, when I suggest that he doesn't know what he is doing, I am failing to honor him and respect him as I should. The issue isn't that I can't state my perspective, it is that I need to do it in the right way with the right attitude.

Day Five Study

Our story this week is about a wife who learned to submit to her husband, who was an unbeliever at the time. Even if you are not married, you will enjoy the lessons she learned about submitting to God, and you will be encouraged in areas where you are learning to submit to others (not my favorite thing to do).

Dolores' Story

I learned to submit to my husband when my marriage was on the rocks and I came to know the Lord through that rough time. I learned to first yield to Jesus as my Savior and Lord of my life. Nothing short of losing my husband, especially to another woman, could have prepared me to yield to Jesus.

My whole life I had planned to have a career. Because I had a crisis pregnancy in high school, I was forced out of school (a parochial school). I got my GED, eventually got my business degree from SMU, and was ready to try to enter the work force when this marital crisis hit. We had a brief separation. When I was invited back into the home, I was told that I would not be able to work outside the house. My biggest dream was crushed, but because of my newfound relationship with the Lord, I looked to Him and said, "Lord, now what? Be a housewife?!!! Give up my idea of being a businesswoman co-equal with men? Okay." I never felt so vulnerable as I did then. I had just gotten my degree and all for naught.

My husband was cold, distant and affectionately unavailable for me. What's more he was still maintaining a friendship with the other woman and her husband. I felt much pain and hurt from those experiences but I learned to lean on Jesus.

I asked the Lord for friendships with other women during this time, but He told me no! He was sufficient. It was during those lonely times that I learned to run to Him whenever trouble hit. He alone was my sufficiency, and I had to learn it without anyone around. This lesson has stood me in good stead. No friend, no counselor, pastor, spiritual advisor was available--only the One that could really do something about my pain and the offensiveness my husband threw my way. Praise God for the crucible. I'm a much stronger person today for it!

I learned not only to submit to God's principles and to my husband but learned that I needed to change. My ever-constant prayer was "Change me, Lord, change me!" I didn't like me because I figured I brought on most of the pain. When I tried to make things better, they backfired, so I concluded that it must be me!

Today I'm learning to submit to things I can't control. I am learning that not everyone will like me nor will they understand me. And that's okay. When I feel unappreciated, ignored or disliked by others, I'm learning to look to God for my comfort. It's amazing how much change that has made in my attitude and in my countenance. It is a freedom from the snare that Satan often has put in my path to steal, kill and destroy my abundant life here and now. Praise God, I'm still a work in progress!

- *Diamonds in the Word*: Summarize what you consider the teaching of the Scriptures on submission. Note the verses where you find the principles, and explain how they support your statements. Make it as simple as possible so that you could use it to help another woman who is in a difficult situation at home or at work.

20. *Sharing question*: As you consider 1 Peter 2:11-3:7, what area of submission is most difficult for you personally? Why?

21. *Sharing question*: Share with your group a specific way that you have found to develop a more gentle and quiet spirit - specific prayers, verses to memorize, Scriptures to read, simply leaving the room, etc.

22. Responding to God: What one specific action will you take this week to become more beautiful in this way? Write it out in the first person, i.e. I will . . ., and remember that God takes us seriously when we say we will do something.

Week Seven: Adorned with Beauty in Unjust Suffering

A Precious Word from God

"Do not return evil for evil or insult for insult,
but instead bless others because you were called to inherit a blessing."
1 Peter 3:9 (NET)

Introduction

We are on the home stretch with our lessons. Hang in there another 3 weeks and you will complete the entire study of 1 Peter. I love the feeling of accomplishment that I get when I put the last touches on a study! If you have missed one or more lessons or days of homework, plan to do them during the period when we aren't meeting. Don't feel defeated but persevere day by day as best you can to finish the entire course.

During the second week of our homework, we looked at the fact that God uses trials of all kinds to refine us into the image of Jesus. In this lesson we consider the specific sufferings that believers face from other people. Some of this is persecution that we encounter. Our sufferings for Christ are generally not as serious as they are for those in some areas of the world. However, we must be faithful to respond to the persecution that we do encounter in God's way. It's not an easy thing to do even if we aren't thrown in prison!

Day One Study

Read 1 Peter 3:8-22.

1. What qualities are we to exhibit according to v. 8?

- *Diamonds in the Word*: Look up the Greek words for these qualities and write down the verse, adding your expanded definitions into the verse.

2. As you can see, v. 8 begins with "finally" (NET) or "to sum up" (NASB). How do vv. 8-12 sum up what we have studied over the past couple of weeks? (You will need to reread 1 Peter 2:11-3:7.)

3. *Sharing question*: Consider each quality that you listed. How are you doing in these areas? Write down an assessment of your progress on each of these separately. For instance, how are you doing on being harmonious (consider it in terms of the relationships that Peter mentioned in 2:13-3:7 and then other relationships as well)? Do this with each specific quality.

4. How does being humble in spirit relate to the other qualities?

5. Responding to God: Write a prayer asking God for the grace to exhibit the qualities of v. 8. Confess to Him where you have fallen short. Pray for your attitude toward specific people with whom you are struggling in these areas.

Day Two Study

Reread 1 Peter 3:8-22.

I intentionally left off the challenge of v. 9 yesterday so that we could deal with it as an independent instruction. It is our "Precious Word from God" for this week. Work on memorizing it. This is one that could come in handy at any time☺

6. Copy v. 9 below to help you memorize it. Why is it such a challenge?

- *Diamonds in the Word*: Peter quotes from Psalm 34:12-16 in 3:10-11. Read the entire Psalm and write down any insights that you have from it.

Usually I don't encounter people who do evil against me personally, but I do almost daily come across a similar type of situation driving in Dallas! According to 1 Peter 3:8, when someone cuts me off, I am not to retaliate. When I get a green light and someone runs the red light on the other side, I am not to get angry and try to hit them (not that I have done this!). I should not make coarse gestures or speak condemning words under my breath. I guess I shouldn't even be honking in anger - this is my usual mode of operation. As a believer, I am not to get angry with those who treat me badly; rather I must see them as God does and treat them as Jesus did those who crucified Him.

7. *Sharing question*: What actions make you want to retaliate - not necessarily driving? How have you returned that treatment in the past?

8. What specific ways to obey vv. 8-9 are given in vv. 10-12?

9. What specific blessings for the one who obeys vv. 8-9 are mentioned in vv. 10-12?

Today words of insult or evil against us would be called verbal abuse if they came from a spouse. Our culture suggests that we have cause to divorce a man who treats us this way.

10. What are we to do instead according to these verses and those in 1 Peter 3:1-6?

♦ *Diamonds in the Word*: Read Matt. 5:43-46. How does it relate to these verses in 1 Pet.?

11. Responding to God: Write a prayer for grace to respond correctly when you encounter insults from anyone. If there is someone in your life who speaks to you this way, pray for the grace of God to respond correctly. This is not an easy obedience. If you have no one like that in your life, think of someone whom you know who is in a hard situation at work or at home and pray for her. Write her a note of encouragement.

Day Three Study

Reread 1 Peter 3:8-22 to put yourself back into the context of these verses.

Peter says we are to keep our tongues from evil (v. 10). That sounds easy until someone speaks hurtful, evil words to us. Our automatic desire is to hurt them back with our words. James has a lot to say about the tongue - its use and its effect upon others.

Read James 3:2-12.

12. With what things does James compare the tongue? What other terms does he use to describe it? How do these help you picture the effects of the tongue?

13. Why are we not to speak to other people with insults and evil according to James 3:9?

14. Peter uses Jesus as our example of how to respond to this kind of treatment in 1 Peter 2:21-23. What do you learn from His example?

15. If we choose to respond in the way that we have been spoken to, what is the consequence according to 1 Peter 3:12? Why is that a scary thought?

16. *Sharing question*: Share with your group some ways that you have learned to seek and pursue peace with those who have mistreated you or ways that you have learned to give a blessing in response to insult. There is no need to mention the specific person with whom you have dealt in this area. Just share how you learned to respond well, not how the other person sinned.

♦ *Diamonds in the Word*: Read Galatians 5:16-26. Relate these verse to 1 Peter 3:8-12.

Day Four Study

Read 1 Peter 3:13-17.

♦ *Diamonds in the Word*: What is the theme of this paragraph? To determine this, ask these questions - What is it primarily about? What ideas are most repeated?

17. Mark in your Bibles the word "suffer" in this paragraph. To what kind of suffering is Peter referring? How do you know?

18. List the responses that Peter suggests for this kind of suffering.

19. *Sharing question*: Have you ever suffered for doing what is right? If so, share the situation and your response with your group. Did you respond as Peter suggests?

Read 1 Peter 3:18-22.

This is a difficult section to understand. There have been a number of interpretations given for it. One thing that has really helped me as I have studied the Bible is to focus on what is clear and what I can learn rather than putting all my interest in the unknown and the strange! God has so much to tell us. We waste a lot of time worrying about the minor areas that are clouded from our perspective today. In heaven we will either learn the truth or we won't care. I tend to believe the latter.

20. What is clear in this passage? How does it reinforce Peter's teaching in vv. 13-17?

- *Diamonds in the Word*: Read a number of commentaries on this passage. Which interpretation seems the most likely to you and why?

21. *Sharing question*: What does it mean to you personally that Jesus died for your sins once for all, meaning for all time? Responding to God: Spend some time praising Jesus for what He has done for you.

Day Five Study

Reread 1 Peter 3:13-4:6.

22. According to 4:1-2, with what purpose are you to arm yourself?

The word "arm" is a military term, so we are preparing for battle by adopting this purpose. Battle terminology is not popular in some quarters of the church anymore. Yet, we are in a battle and must be prepared by being armed with proper weapons.

23. How does Peter describe the lifestyle of the Gentiles? How are they responding to the Christians? Why?

We also face opposition from those with similar attitudes. How are we responding to people who treat us poorly or unfairly? Are we truly reflecting the beauty of Christ in our actions and attitudes? This lesson is not an easy one. I have not mastered it in any way. Only by the grace and power of God can we respond as Peter has challenged us to do.

Mary's Story

Rosie was my husband's mother. My husband and I only dated 3 months prior to getting married and I had only met his mother twice prior to our marriage. Nothing could have prepared me for Rosie.

Rosie had grown up in a household of physical abuse from both her father and her brothers. She had married my husband's dad to get away from home, but he was also physically abusive. She had a total of 7 children, one of whom died, within the course of 9 years before she and her husband were divorced. My husband was the oldest of these children. As a single mom of 6 children, she took in boarders and ironing in order to keep food on the table for her children. She was a very insecure and angry mother, who took out her fears and frustrations both verbally and physically on her children. However, her children became her life and she became a very controlling mother. She eventually remarried and was married to her second husband for 23 years. That marriage ended tragically as well, leaving her more insecure and angry.

Rosie had 5 boys and 1 girl. She was very protective and controlling of all of her children, and she was also very jealous of their affections for others. My husband was the oldest of her sons, so she felt betrayed when he married me and we moved into our own home several miles away from her. It was not uncommon for her to call our house 10 to 12 times per day. Many of the conversations were angry outbursts.

I found it very difficult to love Rosie. I did not have a personal relationship with the Lord during the early days of my marriage so my response to her was not Christ like. Rosie knew the Lord but did not know His word. Her faith was based on a mixture of truth and false teaching. As God began to work in my life and I surrendered to Him in faith, He began to deal with me about my relationship with Rosie.

In my husband's family, if someone became ill, the assumption was that they needed to be left alone until they were healed. Therefore, if they were in the hospital, no one visited them until time to bring them home. My family was the opposite. If someone was in the hospital, one or more members of my family stayed with them until they came home. Rosie became ill and was in the hospital for a week. Every morning on my way to work I would stop at the hospital and pick up and deliver fresh laundry to her. I would visit with her on my way home from work. She was so stunned by my attention. I had no thoughts that I was serving the Lord or building a relationship with her; I was merely doing what came naturally. However, the Lord used that time of her hospitalization to develop our relationship with each other. It was during this time that we began to love each other. She seemed to be able to let go of her jealousies related to my husband and began to view us as one. I loved her and treated her with a godly love, but still in my heart there was always the wariness based on the early days of our relationship and her explosiveness. I really had no idea how much I truly loved her until she died.

She lived to be 93 years old. I had known her for 30 years when she died. I received a phone call on Feb. 10, 2001 telling me that she had fallen and hit her head. Before I could get to the hospital, she had died. The death certificate said she had had a stroke prior to her fall. To this day, I miss her phone calls and wish that I could hear her voice again. Maybe, if I could start over, I would not resent the interruptions and her telling me what preacher to watch on television but would be more tolerant. I wish I could have told her how much I loved her before she died. I wonder if we will be able to tell one another we love each other when we get to heaven.

24. *Sharing question*: Who is your Rosie? Who speaks evil of you or insults you? To whom do you have trouble responding with the beauty of Jesus? Carry with you a copy of our verse this week and pull it out when you know that you will be encountering this difficult and unlovable person.

25. Responding to God: Talk to God about this difficult person. Confess your failures in treating her or him with blessing, harmony, and sympathy. Pray for the person in positive ways rather than merely complaining. Thank God for one positive trait in that individual. Ask Him for the beauty of Jesus in your response next time you see her/him.

Week Eight: Adorned with Beauty, Knowing the End Is Near

A Precious Word from God

"Above all keep your love for one another fervent,
because love covers a multitude of sins"
1 Peter 4:8 (NET)

Introduction

The end is near - words that should affect the way we live our lives today. What we truly believe should do more than merely give us head knowledge. It should cause us to see the present with different eyes. We have already recognized that we are aliens on this earth because our real home is heaven. Now we hear that Jesus' return is near! Are you ready?

Day One Study

In 1 Peter 4:7, Peter announces to these first century Christians that the end is near. From our perspective, it looks like he was wrong. After all, it has been two thousand years. That doesn't seem too near! So what do we do? Do we discount his words and believe that the end is not really near at all and that we can continue our lives as usual?

1. Read 2 Peter 3:3-9. In light of these verses, explain Peter's words that the end is near and yet we are still waiting for it after 2000 years.

Read 1 Peter 4:7-19.

2. What adjustments does Peter suggest for the believer's life in light of the fact that the end is near (vv. 7-11)?

- *Diamonds in the Word*: Look up the Greek for "sound judgment" (NASB) or "self-controlled" (NET) and "sober-minded" (NET) or "sober spirit" in v. 7. What insights do you gain about prayer?

3. *Sharing question*: What part does prayer play in your life? How would that change if you truly believed that the end is near?

4. Read 1 John 3:2-3. If you truly look forward to seeing the Lord, what will you do about it according to John?

5. *Sharing question*: What difference does it make to you in a practical sense that soon you will be going to your real home? How does that affect your life on a day-to-day basis? If it doesn't make any practical difference to you, what plan can you implement to change that?

Day Two Study

Reread 1 Peter 4:7-19.

1 Peter 4:8 is our Precious Word from God this week. I hope you are doing well with your memorization of these verses. Peter prefaces his instruction in this verse with the phrase, "above all." Apparently this is an extremely important command in light of the fact that the end is near. In Day One of Week Three, on pp. 22-23, we looked at another command about love in 1 Peter 1:22. Please reread the verse, and you can review your study if you like.

6. Compare the two instructions about love. What does the command in 4:8 add to what Peter already said in 1:22?

The word for love here in 4:8 is *agape*, the same love that God has for us. Dr. Zodhiates says that *agape* means "benevolent love. Its benevolence, however, is not shown by doing what the person loved desires but what the one who loves deems as needed by the one loved. . . but for man to show love to God, he must first appropriate God's *agape*, for only God has such an unselfish love."[11]

7. *Sharing question*: If you are a parent, how does love look and act when your child sins? If you are not a parent, how did your parents' love respond when you disobeyed?

8. In light of the definition of godly love, explain how love might cover a multitude of sins. Does that mean that we just overlook sin in the lives of others - live and let live?

Read James 5:16-20.

9. What practical ways from these verses do you see that you are to love someone and therefore cover a multitude of sins?

---

[11] Spiros Zodhiates, *The Complete Word Study New Testament* (Chattanooga, TN: AMG Publishers, 1991), 866.

10. *Sharing question*: When have you so loved someone that you tried to turn them back from the error of their ways? Share with your group what happened and the outcome.

In 1 Peter 4:9 we are instructed to "show hospitality to one another without complaining." At the time of Peter's writing, believers had to open their homes as churches and also for traveling apostles and evangelists. We see in the book of Acts that Paul went from city to city proclaiming the gospel and staying with various families. Many of his letters record the names of the hosts of the house church in those cities. Our culture does not require that kind of hospitality; however, this instruction does apply to us as well. What is keeping you from hosting other believers at your home to build relationships?

- *Diamonds in the Word*: Do one or both of the following: 1. Go through the verses at the end of Paul's epistles (and the beginning of Philemon), looking for references to the hosts/ hostesses of home churches. 2. Read through the book of Acts and write down the times when someone shows hospitality to one of God's workers. How does this encourage you to show hospitality?

I used to go to such beautiful homes owned by people in my church that I was ashamed of my humble home. Then, God began to work on me; He showed me that He had given me what I had. It belonged to Him, not to me. It was a mansion compared to the homes of the great majority of people in this world. God's Spirit convicted me that my sin of pride was the problem, not the house. So I began to open my home for fellowships and for meetings, etc. I have always received the greatest blessing from doing so.

11. *Sharing question*: How can you apply 1 Peter 4:8 personally?

Day Three Study

Reread 1 Peter 4:7-19.

In our study today we are going to look at spiritual gifts in a very surface way. It would take us several weeks to study this in-depth. If you have never really studied this subject, you might want to do some study on your own during the weeks after this class concludes or do the *Diamonds in the Word* assignment.

12. Why would Peter mention spiritual gifts in context of the approaching end of all things?

13. Write down what you learn about gifts in vv. 10-11.
    a. Who has received them?
    b. How are they to be used (v. 10)?

c. What 2 areas of gifts are mentioned in v. 11 and how are you to use them?

d. What is the outcome as we use our gifts (v.11)?

- *Diamonds in the Word*: Look up the other three passages that deal with spiritual gifts - 1 Cor. 12-14, Romans 12:1-8; Eph. 4:7-16 - and write down the principles that you learn about spiritual gifts in general. Try to answer observations questions of who, what, where, when, why, and how about spiritual gifts.

14. *Sharing question*: If you are God's steward, what does that mean in a practical way concerning your spiritual gifts?

Read Matthew 25:14-30. This parable is about money, not spiritual gifts, but the principles apply to any kind of stewardship.

15. What do you learn from this parable about managing God's resources?

16. *Sharing question*: How are you doing as a steward of God's gifts, especially spiritual gifts? How can you begin to use your gifts in your church, as God intends that you do?

17. Responding to God: You may need to confess that you have not been a good steward of the gifts that God has given you. You may want to ask God to show you the right area of service. Thank Him for being so gracious that He wants to use you in His mighty work. Tell Him that you want to show His beauty as you use His gifts.

Day Four Study

Reread 1 Peter 4:12-19.

Again, Peter comes back to the problem of suffering as a Christian.

18. What attitudes are we to have when we experience this kind of suffering according to this passage?

19. What parallels do you see in this passage and those we have previously considered in 1 Peter that deal with suffering?

- *Diamonds in the Word*: Look up the Greek words for "sufferings" (NET; NASB) in v. 13 and "suffer" in v. 15. Look up all the other New Testament references that use those words. What insights do you gain about suffering?

20. Peter calls this suffering a "trial by fire." How do you see this kind of suffering parallel a fire?

21. In vv. 17-18 Peter mentions judgment for believers. Considering the context and Romans 8:1, what is he talking about? What is this judgment?

22. *Sharing question*: Are you prepared for suffering as a believer or do you shy away from any situation where you may endure hostility from unbelievers? Can you think of a situation where you need to be up front about your faith although you risk facing a negative reaction?

Day Five Study

As we conclude this week's study, we need to consider it from the standpoint of keeping an eternal perspective on all things. When we do that, we become more beautiful because we see ourselves, our ministries, and our sufferings through the eyes of God and respond with grace. Keep this in mind as you reread this passage.

Reread 1 Peter 4:7-19.

23. *Sharing question*: In what area of your life would you be more beautiful if you had an eternal perspective? How can you better focus on the eternal each day?

24. *Sharing question*: How did you learn what your spiritual gifts are? Share with your group some practical things that helped you identify where God wanted you to serve. If you do not know what your gifts are, ask God for direction.

This week's story is from a woman who had an open heart to serve God and His church. She was willing to do whatever she was asked and in the process learned that she has the gift of administration, which blesses people even in her workplace.

Diane's Story

The coordinator for our Christmas Luncheon asked me to be her assistant in 2000, and after it was over, she and our Minister to Women were talking and hinting that I would be a good one to take it over. I said, "No, I like to stay in the background." Our Minister to Women grinned with a gleam in her eye and said nothing further.

Several months later at work, I was given a supervisory position, the first one in thirteen years. It turned out to be okay - the seven or eight folks assigned to me worked on various projects, so I didn't really have to lead them too much. It turned out to be a nice safe way to take on more responsibility.

In January 2002, the Chairman of the Women's Ministry Board offered me the choice of either coordinating the Christmas Luncheon or the retreat. I prayed about it and realized that I could do the Christmas Luncheon without feeling too dependent on God, because I knew how that was "supposed" to work, whereas with the retreat, I had no idea, because I had not been involved in any of the planning for that in the past. I knew that I would have to depend a whole bunch more on God and that was probably a good thing for me. So I accepted.

In April of 2003 I became a project manager at work (instead of doing specialized work on various projects).

It just seems that God is leading me through various roles to grow me and show me how to serve His church.

25. *Sharing question*: We have covered a number of topics this week - spiritual gifts, suffering, hospitality, love, and prayer. How has God spoken to you about your life specifically? Responding to God: Respond to His Spirit's prompting in prayer.

Week Nine: Adorned with the Beauty of Humility

A Precious Word from God

"And God will exalt you in due time, if you humble yourselves under his mighty hand by casting all your cares on Him because He cares for you."
1 Peter 5:6-7 (NET)

Introduction

We are on the home stretch of our study of 1 Peter. I hope that God has used it in your life in mighty ways. I have been praying that He would adorn us as women as we apply the truths that we have seen. I know that God has shown me areas of my own life where I need to be changed within as I have worked through Peter's letter. Because God has promised that His Word does not return to Him void without accomplishing the work that He sent it to do (Isaiah 55:11), I know that He has used it in your life over these weeks that we have spent together. I thank Him for all that He has accomplished in making us more beautiful women.

Day One Study

Read 1 Peter 5.

We are going to come back to vv. 1-4 tomorrow. Right now we are focusing on the verses that are specifically addressed to everyone.

1. List all the instructions given in vv. 5-10.

The first two instructions concern humility. What is humility?

2. If you have a Greek concordance, look up the word and its definition in the Greek. If you don't, at least check an English dictionary, understanding that the Greek definition was the one that Peter used when he wrote this letter. Write out the two instructions with the expanded definition in them. What insights do you gain?

3. Why is humility important according to v. 5?

- *Diamonds in the Word*: Study humility in the Scriptures and its opposite, pride. Look in your concordance for references to these two qualities and look up as many verses as you can within your time constraints. Write down your insights about humility.

4. How did Jesus humble Himself according to Phil. 2:5-8? What do you learn from Him about humility?

5. *Sharing question*: How do you obey these instructions concerning humility? Give at least one specific thing that you can do in your situation to be like Jesus in this way.

Day Two Study

Today we are going back to the first few verses of 1 Peter 5, written to the elders of the church. In some churches there is an actual board of elders. In other churches, the pastors are considered to be the elders. The issue in this context is not exactly what form this takes but how they should rule.

Reread 1 Peter 5.

6. What specific instructions does Peter give to the elders (vv. 1-4)? What promise?

7. What general principles of leadership do you see in these verses, which are written specifically to the elders but also apply to all leaders in our churches?

8. How do these principles relate to the instructions on humility that follow it? Why would they be mentioned together?

9. *Sharing question*: Where are you a leader either within or without the church, perhaps even in your home or your job? Can you apply these principles in any way to that position, whether it is an actual assigned position or a place where you influence others? If so, how?

- *Diamonds in the Word*: In Numbers 12:3 Moses is described as the most humble man on the earth and yet he was a great leader. Study his life, and consider what you learn from him about humility and leadership.

10. Responding to God: Talk to God about humility and leadership. Is there an area of your life where you are not proving to be an example to others?

Day Three Study

Reread 1 Peter 5:5-11.

11. *Sharing question*: We already saw that Peter gives three instructions about dealing with the devil. Write for each one of the three a specific action that you might take to obey it.

- *Diamonds in the Word*: Study in a Bible dictionary or encyclopedia and write down what you learn about the devil. Be sure and look up the verses listed and write down where this information is given in the Scriptures.

12. What is happening in the lives of the believers to whom Peter is writing that made them susceptible to the devil (v. 9-10)? What similarities do you see to situations in which lions may attack?

13. To what promises are the believers to hold onto (v. 10)? How does this parallel other promises in 1 Peter concerning suffering? Review 1 Peter, and write down specific similarities.

14. How do humility, suffering, and the devil relate? When different subjects are put together in the same context, we always need to think about their relationship. What would make Peter think of them at the same time?

15. *Sharing question*: In what circumstances are you most vulnerable to attack from the devil? What can you apply from the book of 1 Peter to make you stronger and less open to attack?

16. Responding to God: Ask God for the grace to obey the instructions in 1 Peter 5. Describe your feelings about the areas where you are struggling with temptation. Ask for the strength to stand firm against the devil.

Day Four Study

Reread 1 Peter 5:5-11.

Review the three instructions concerning the devil. Today we will consider some examples of dealing with temptation as well as considering some of the devil's tactics so that we are able to resist, etc.

17. Compare James 4:6-10 with this 1 Peter passage. Give any insights that you gain about dealing with Satan.

- *Diamonds in the Word*: What biblical story would you use to help women understand how to deal with temptation? Write down the basic plot and the applications that you see.

18. Read these passage and write down what do you learn about dealing with temptation:

    a. James 1:13-18

    b. 2 Timothy 2:22

    c. Matt. 4:1-11

    d. Matthew 16:21-23

Day Five Study

There is no question that we are not beautiful when we fall into sin. Laura shares her story of how she applied 2 Timothy 2:22 when she was tempted to sin.

Laura's Story

I was single and working. I was attracted to a non-believer at work. We had gone out as friends a few times. We went on a road trip that was supposed to be a group, but it worked out just being the two of us to see a college football game. We ended up kissing. We had to figure out a way to go back to work and just be friends. However, I was hooked. We were friends, and I had kissed him. I had strong feelings for him.

The Lord kept telling me he was the wrong man for me. Finally, I decided to obey and leave this guy alone. However, it wasn't easy. I was attracted to him, I worked with him, and I had the memory of his kiss.

One day at work, I started dwelling on the situation. I was overcome with desire and wanted to pursue the relationship. However, instead I left the office at lunch. I drove my car to a bus stop parking lot and read 1 Thess. 4:1-7 over and over. I prayed. I asked the Lord to help me overcome the desire I was experiencing. That is exactly what happened. I went back to work and the power of God's word helped me not act on my temptation that day.

19. *Sharing question*: Relate your own story of a time when you were tempted and how you stood firm instead.

Sometimes our temptation is not to sin in an overt way like our story, but to distrust God. Romans 14:23b says, "Whatever is not from faith is sin." Whenever we decide that God is out to get us, is not good, is not faithful to His promises, etc., we are sinning because we are failing to trust Him.

Much of 1 Peter deals with trials, with suffering and persecution. In the midst of all of that, sometimes Satan encourages us to turn from God. Here is a story of a woman who went through a trial and trusted God in the midst of it and ended up with great blessing.

Janie's Story

I would say that my life has always gone pretty close to plan for what I wanted to happen. Probably the only hitch in that plan was not finding my husband until I was 35. But that's another story.

I had been a Christian since I was 11. However, I realize now that because things were fairly easy, there was not a reason for me to feel a deep dependence on the Lord. After we married within a year of knowing each other, we wanted to wait awhile to have children. So at age 38 or 39 we started "trying." (That phrase has always cracked me up, but what else do you say?) After several months without success, I talked with my gynecologist, and we began the blood tests and things that you do to make sure that your body is functioning the way it is supposed to. Then, it was time to make an appointment with an infertility doctor. After waiting two months for the appointment and another hour in the waiting room, we went in to see him where he talked with us between mouthfuls of a late-lunch hamburger. We weren't feeling so great about this path.

So, we tried another doctor who happened to have a cancellation fairly soon and he was very nice. All the while we were praying for God to let us have a family. We had not talked about adoption - it was not even a consideration at this stage. But somewhere in the back of my mind, I was afraid that that was where God was leading us.

With infertility treatments, you make a plan - we'll do this for x months and then evaluate where we want to go next. The pills were ok, but the shots were a real drag. Everything had to be timed perfectly. Once when my husband was out of town and I needed a shot at midnight, my dad came over to my house at midnight and gave me a shot. I always thought I was a strong person and knew that God gives me the strength I need to handle any situation, but this was starting to push it. We lived in two week cycles from ovulation to menstrual cycle and at the sign of my period would come a huge let down. Tears together brought us closer and more in love.

We had been bearing the load ourselves and had only told a few people about what was going on. My small group Bible Study was a great comfort, and knowing that they were praying was a big support. The feelings were embarrassing, admitting failure at something and an acknowledgement that everything was not ok. All these things I am well acquainted with now, but at that time did not want to share. Plus, it was so difficult and painful that it was like a constant open wound.

As I grew closer to that magic age of 40 every day, I began to think of other options. There had been some things in the news about international adoption, and my heart was touched that there were so many children who would never have a home. When I mentioned this to my husband, he seemed open to the idea. We went on a hot summer day to The Gladney Center in Ft. Worth - armed with questions from all the horror stories we had read on the Internet about international adoption. After the meeting, we felt encouraged and wanted to seriously consider that path. We began to pray that God would show us His plan. We set one more treatment as the last one and if it worked, great. If it didn't, then we would adopt. When something happened with my body that I could not complete the treatment, I told the doctor's office that we would not pursue more.

That night, we went to dinner with friends. I felt giddy from the freedom I felt to be free of the infertility treatments and excited about God's plan for adoption. The process to adopt our son took about six months total. All along the way, God was starting to work on my heart to be free to give Him the credit. He was providing the avenue to give Him the glory. And today, because of the way our family was formed, I still have the opportunity to prove my faith when I talk about how God is the one who brings families together.

I used to feel awkward about how to put God in a conversation. But the work that He has done in my heart through this trial and the growth that happened as a result makes giving Him the glory natural. He changes hearts, and rich spiritual blessings come from trusting in Him to work all things together for good.

In writing this story, it has been somewhat difficult to pull up the pain of the trial. Isn't it interesting that the way that God works so often is that he erases the painful details when they are no longer needed? One thing I have seen so clearly in this is that when God does a work, He does it COMPLETELY. I praise God every day for the beautiful gift of my children - that His thoughts are not our thoughts, and His ways are not our ways.

20. *Sharing question*: When we lack faith, we sin. What are some ways that the devil tempts you to distrust God or to act independently of Him? What have you learned this week to help you stand firm against this?

21. Responding to God: Write a prayer asking for God's grace and strength in the area of your greatest temptation or the area where you are doubting His love, etc. Think of a specific way that you need to avoid the situation or the sin or of ways to grow in faith rather than unbelief.

The NET BIBLE® is an extraordinary new translation of the Bible with 60,932 translators' notes provided by the ministry of bible.org. These translators' notes make the original meaning of the Bible far more accessible by unlocking the riches of the Bible's truth from entirely new perspectives.

The NET BIBLE® is the first modern Bible to be completely free for anyone anywhere in the world to download. The pioneering "Ministry First" approach at bible.org seeks to remove money as a barrier for great ministry. Learn more online at www.bible.org/ministryfirst.

About bible.org

Bible.org is a non-profit (501c3) Christian ministry headquartered in Dallas, Texas. In the last decade, bible.org has grown to serve millions of individuals around the world and provides thousands of trustworthy resources for Bible study including the new NET BIBLE® translation.

Resources Available

Bible.org offers thousands of free resources for:

- ✞ Women's Ministry
- ✞ Men's Ministry
- ✞ Pastoral Helps
- ✞ Small Group Curriculum and much more...

Go to www.bible.org for thousands of free trustworthy Bible study resources including:

- The NET BIBLE®
- The NeXt Bible Learning Environment™ - the most powerful new online Bible search and study tool on the internet today
- Spiritual formation and discipleship materials
- Theological training materials
- Bible commentaries and dictionaries
- More than 10,000 sermon illustrations
- More than 4,000 resources for Bible study

Download the entire NET BIBLE® and 60,932 notes for free at www.bible.org

Made in the USA
Columbia, SC
14 January 2022